Dr Melanie Fennell is an internationally recognize
practitioner and trainer. She is Director of an Advance
course based at Oxford Cognitive Therapy Centre an
She is a recognized expert in low self-esteem and has run workshops and
presented papers at major international conferences.

The Overcoming series was initiated by Peter Cooper, Professor of
Psychology at the University of Reading and Honorary NHS Consultant
Clinical Psychologist. His original book on bulimia nervosa and binge-
eating founded the series in 1993 and continues to help many thousands
of people in the USA, the UK and Europe. The aim of the series is to help
people with a wide range of common problems and disorders to take
control of their own recovery programme using the latest techniques
of cognitive behavioural therapy. Each book, with its specially tailored
programme, is devised by a practising clinician. Many books in the Overcoming series are now recommended by the UK Department of Health
under the Books on Prescription scheme.

Other titles in the Overcoming series:

OVERCOMING
LOW SELF-ESTEEM
SELF-HELP COURSE

A 3-part programme based on Cognitive Behavioural Techniques

Part One: Understanding Low Self-Esteem

Melanie Fennell

ROBINSON
London

Constable & Robinson Ltd
3 The Lanchesters
162 Fulham Palace Road
London W6 9ER
www.overcoming.co.uk

First published in the UK by Robinson,
an imprint of Constable & Robinson Ltd 2006

Important Note

This book is not intended as a substitute for medical advice or treatment.
Any person with a condition requiring medical attention should consult
a qualified medical practitioner or suitable therapist.

ISBN 13: 978-1-84529-237-9 (Pack ISBN)
ISBN 10: 1-84529-237-5

ISBN 13: 978-1-84529-392-5 (Part One)
ISBN 10: 1-84529-392-4

ISBN 13: 978-1-84529-393-2 (Part Two)
ISBN 10: 1-84529-393-2

ISBN 13: 978-1-84529-394-9 (Part Three)
ISBN 10: 1-84529-394-0

3 5 7 9 10 8 6 4 2

Printed and bound in the EU

Introduction: How to Use this Workbook

This is a self-help course for dealing with low self-esteem. It has two aims:

1 To help you develop a better understanding of the problem

2 To teach you the practical skills you will need in order to change

How the course works

The *Overcoming Low Self-Esteem Self-Help Course* will help you understand how low self-esteem develops and what keeps it going, and then to make changes in your life so that you begin to feel more confident and more kindly and accepting towards yourself.

These workbooks are designed to help you work, either by yourself or with your healthcare practitioner, to overcome low self-esteem. With plenty of questionnaires, charts, worksheets and practical exercises, the three parts together make up a structured course.

Part One explains:

- What low self-esteem is

- How low self-esteem affects people

- How negative experiences affect people

- What keeps low self-esteem going

Part Two explains:

- How to recognize and deal with anxious predictions

- How to recognize and question self-critical thoughts

- How to identify your positive qualities

- How to gain a balanced view of yourself and start enjoying life

Part Three explains:

- What Rules for Living are

- How to change your Rules for Living

- How to recognize and change your central belief about yourself

- How to draft and fine-tune an Action Plan for the future

How long will the course take?

Each workbook will take at least two or three weeks to work through – but do not worry if you feel that you need to give each one extra time. Some things can be understood and changed quite quickly, but others take longer. You will know when you are ready to move on to the next workbook. Completing the entire course could take only two to three months, but this will depend on how quickly you wish to work. Take your time, and go at the pace that suits you best.

Getting the most from the course

Here are some tips to help you get the most from the workbooks:

- These workbooks are not priceless antiques – they are practical tools. So feel free not only to write on the worksheets and charts, but also to underline and highlight things, and to write comments and questions in the margins. By the time you have finished with a workbook, it should look well and truly used.

- You will also find lots of space in the main text. This is for you to write down your thoughts and ideas, and your responses to the questions.

- Keep an open mind and be willing to experiment with new ideas and skills. These workbooks will sometimes ask you to think about painful issues. However, if low self-esteem is distressing you and restricting your life, it really is worth making the effort to overcome it. The rewards will be substantial.

- Be prepared to invest time in doing the practical exercises – set aside 20 to 30 minutes each day if you can.

- Try to answer all the questions and do the exercises, even if you have to come back to some of them later. There may be times when you get stuck and can't think how to take things forward. If this happens, don't get angry with yourself or give up. Just put the workbook aside and come back to it later, when you are feeling more relaxed.

- You may find it helpful to work through the workbooks with a friend. Two heads are often better than one. And you may be able to encourage each other to persist, even when one of you is finding it hard.

- Use the Thoughts and Reflections section at the back of the workbook to write down anything you read that has been particularly helpful to you.

- Re-read the workbook. You may get more out of it once you've had a chance to think about some of the ideas and put them into practice for a little while.

- Each workbook builds on what has already been covered. So what you learn when working with one will help you when you come to the next. It's quite possible simply to dip into different ones as you please, but you may get most out of the series if you follow them through systematically, step by step.

A note of caution

These workbooks will not help everyone who has low self-esteem. If you find that focusing on self-esteem is actually making you feel worse instead of better, or if your negative beliefs about yourself are so strong that you cannot even begin to use the ideas and practical skills described, you may be suffering from clinical depression. The recognized signs of clinical depression include:

- Constantly feeling sad, down, depressed or empty

- General lack of interest in what's going on around you

- A big increase or decrease in your appetite and weight

- A marked change in your sleep patterns

- Noticeable speeding up or slowing down in your movements and how you go about things

- Feeling of being tired and low in energy

- An intense sense of guilt or worthlessness

- Difficulty in concentrating and making decisions

- A desire to hurt yourself or a feeling that you might be better off dead

If you have had five or more of these symptoms (including low mood or loss of interest) for two weeks or more, you should seek professional help from a doctor, counsellor or psychotherapist. There is nothing shameful about seeking this sort of professional help – any more than there is anything shameful about taking your car to a garage if it is not working as it should, or going to see a lawyer if you have legal problems. It simply means taking your journey towards self-knowledge and self-acceptance with the help of a friendly guide, rather than striking out alone.

SECTION 1: What is Low Self-Esteem?

This section will help you to understand:

- what low self-esteem is
- whether you have low self-esteem
- how we develop beliefs about ourselves
- how low self-esteem affects a person
- how low self-esteem affects our lives
- how low self-esteem is linked to other problems
- how the impact of low self-esteem varies

What is low self-esteem?

Self-esteem refers to the overall beliefs or opinions we have about ourselves, and the value we place on ourselves as people. A person with low self-esteem will have generally negative self-beliefs.

Look at the following statements and write 'N' next to the ones that sound negative.

a 'I am comfortable with myself as I am.' _____

b 'I'm useless.' _____ No

c 'Nothing I do matters.' ___N__

d 'I'm a good person.' _____

e 'The things I do are worthwhile.' ___N__

f 'I'm worthless.' ___N__

g 'I am weak and inferior to other people.' ___N__

h 'I appreciate and respect myself.' _____

i 'I'm important to the people around me.' _____

j 'I dislike myself.' _____

k 'No one cares about me.' _____

Do any of the negative statements sound familiar? Perhaps you have had some of these feelings yourself? To find out more, work through the next exercise.

Do I have low self-esteem?

Take a look at the ten statements below. Put a tick next to each question in the column that best reflects how you feel about yourself. Be honest – there are no right or wrong answers, simply tell the truth about how you see yourself.

	Yes, definitely	Yes, mostly	Yes, sometimes	No, mostly	No, not at all
My experience in life has taught me to value and appreciate myself				✓	
I have a good opinion of myself					✓
I treat myself well and look after myself properly					✓
I like myself					✓
I give as much weight to my qualities, skills, assets and strengths as I do to my weaknesses and flaws					✓
I feel good about myself					✓
I feel I am entitled to other people's attention and time					✓
I believe I am entitled to the good things in life					✓
My expectations of myself are no more rigid or exacting than my expectations of other people					✓
I am kind and encouraging towards myself, rather than self-critical					✓

If your answers to these statements are not mainly 'Yes, definitely', then this book could be useful to you. If you're troubled by self-doubt, if your thoughts about yourself are often unkind and critical, or if you have difficulty in feeling that you have any true worth or that you deserve happiness, these are signs that your self-esteem is low. And low self-esteem may be having a painful and damaging effect on your life.

How does low self-esteem affect a person?

Negative beliefs about ourselves can be expressed in many ways (such as how we look and behave) and it's useful to learn how to recognize these outward signs.

If you think you have low self-esteem, you could consider yourself at this point. But you may find it more helpful to start by thinking about someone you know who you consider has low self-esteem. This is because, when we try to look at ourselves, it is often difficult to get a clear view – we are too close to the problem.

Think about the person you have chosen. Remember in as much detail as you can a recent time when you met. You may find it helpful to think of more than one person so a blank worksheet has been provided at the back of the book for you to use.

1 **What did you talk about?** (Did he or she express a lot of self-criticism, self-blame or self-doubt?)

_____Yes_____

_____

_____

_____

2 **How did the person behave?** (Did he or she sit hunched over, looking down? Did he or she speak in a hushed voice, or avoid making eye contact? Did you have the feeling he or she was putting on a front – working hard to appear cheerful, for example, or being the life and soul of the party instead of relaxing and being natural?)

_____Yes_____

_____

_____

_____

3 **What sort of mood was the person in?** (For example, did he or she seem shy, sad, anxious, ashamed, frustrated or angry?)

Sad

4 **How was the person's body state?** (For example, did he or she seem tired or tense?)

tired

This exercise shows how low self-esteem (negative beliefs about the self) can affect thinking, behaviour, emotions and body sensations. Now that you have got an idea of what to look out for, imagine observing yourself in the same way. What would be the signs of low self-esteem in _your_ case?

Thoughts:

Behaviour:

_____

_____

Emotions:

_____

_____

_____

_____

Body state:

_____

_____

_____

_____

How does low self-esteem affect our lives?

Just as low self-esteem is reflected in many aspects of a person, so it has an impact on many areas of life.

Tick the statements below that most closely match the way you feel.

Work

☑ **a** 'I work late nearly every night, but I still don't get half the things done I need to.'

☑ **b** 'My parents are disappointed that I haven't done better.'

☐ **c** 'I put in as much as I have to do for my work and no more. I sometimes think I could do something more demanding, but I'm a bit worried about having to learn new skills.'

☑ **d** 'I thought about applying for a new job but I know I probably won't get it, so I'm better off staying where I am.'

Personal relationships

☑ **a** 'If someone criticizes something I do, I always feel terrible.'

☑ **b** 'I'm not very good in a group of people – I can't think what to say and often blush or stammer when I start to speak.'

☑ **c** 'I sometimes find myself apologizing for something that wasn't actually my fault.'

☐ **d** 'I usually drink too much at social events. If I didn't, I'd probably just stand in a corner feeling shy and awkward.'

Self-care

☐ **a** 'I know I ought to take time off work when I'm sick, but I worry that I'll let my workmates down.'

☑ **b** 'My hair's a mess and I could do with some new clothes.'

☐ **c** 'I smoke a lot, especially when I'm stressed out or a bit down.'

☑ **d** 'People tell me I obsess about the way I look but I'm worried about not being as attractive as possible all the time.'

Leisure activities

☑ **a** 'I know I ought to do more exercise but I don't dare join my local gym because everyone else there is really fit.'

☑ **b** 'I'd like to join an art class but I don't have any talent so I'd just make a fool of myself.'

☑ **c** 'I'd love to have a facial or a massage but I'd feel guilty about spending money on myself.'

☑ **d** 'I find it hard to sit down and relax – there's always something that needs doing in the house.'

Now let's look at your answers and see how low self-esteem may be affecting your life.

Work

If you ticked **a** or **b** you may be a real perfectionist and relentlessly work yourself hard. Nothing is good enough. You may not give yourself credit for your achievements or believe that good results come from your own skill and abilities.

If you ticked **c** or **d** you may have a pattern of avoiding challenges for fear of failing. People with low self-esteem often perform below their potential.

Personal relationships

If you ticked **a** you may be oversensitive to criticism and disapproval.

If you ticked **b** you may suffer from extreme self-consciousness, which may stop you expressing yourself. It could even make you want to back away from social situations altogether.

If you ticked **c** you may be so eager to please that you always put others first, no matter what the cost to yourself.

If you ticked **d** you may try to appear lively and confident but, underneath, you worry that if you don't behave in this way people will find you boring and won't want to know you.

Self-care

If you ticked **a**, **b** or **c** then you may not take proper care of yourself because you don't feel that you deserve to be looked after.

If you ticked **d** you may spend hours perfecting every detail of how you look, convinced that this is the only way to be attractive to other people.

Leisure activities

If you ticked **a** or **b** you may avoid any leisure activity in which there is a risk of being judged.

If you ticked **c** or **d** you may have an underlying belief that you do not deserve rewards, treats or any time to relax and enjoy yourself.

How is low self-esteem linked to other problems?

Low self-esteem is sometimes **a consequence of** other problems, such as:

- relationship difficulties

- financial hardship

- severe stress

- chronic pain or illness

- panic attacks

All these problems can undermine confidence and lead to loss of self-esteem. In this case, tackling the root problem may provide the most effective solution. People who learn to manage panic attacks, for example, often regain their confidence without needing to do much work on low self-esteem in its own right. If this is your situation, you may still find some useful ideas in these workbooks to help you restore your belief in yourself. It could also be worth consulting other titles in the 'Overcoming' series to see whether any of them address your problems directly.

Sometimes low self-esteem can be **a factor contributing to** other problems, such as:

- depression

- suicidal thoughts

- eating disorders (e.g. anorexia or binge-eating)

- extreme shyness

If the difficulties you are currently having seem to spring from an underlying sense of low self-esteem, then working on your current problems (e.g. depression or shyness) may be useful but is unlikely to produce real changes in your view of yourself. To make lasting changes, you probably need to tackle the issue of low self-esteem in its own right. In this case, you could benefit greatly from using this workbook as a guide to working on your beliefs about yourself, undermining the old negative views and building up new, more helpful perspectives.

How does the impact of low self-esteem vary?

You may be a person who is generally self-confident but suffers from occasional moments of self-doubt in particularly challenging situations. Or you may be someone who is constantly tormented by self-criticism and finds it hard to think of anything good about yourself. Or of course you may be somewhere in between these two extremes.

Imagine how you would feel in the following situations and put a cross on the line, between 0 (calm and confident) and 10 (extremely anxious):

1 You are about to be interviewed for a new job.

0_____5_____ 10

2 You are asking someone out for a first date.

0_____5_____ 10

3 You have been invited to a big party where you will know only a few people.

0_____5_____ 10

4 You have been sold a defective product and you need to get a refund from the supplier.

0_____5_____ 10

5 Someone who works for your firm has been coming in late every day and you have to reprimand him or her.

0_____5_____ 10

If most of your crosses are towards the extreme left, your self-doubt is probably only triggered in certain situations and you can generally manage it without serious distress or difficulty. When you have difficulties in life, you usually see them as problems to be solved, rather than as a sign that there is something fundamentally wrong with you as a person. You have some positive views about yourself, which balance out self-doubt triggered by challenging situations. These workbooks may have limited relevance for you, though they could still be useful in helping to fine-tune an already strong sense of self-confidence.

If most of your crosses are towards the extreme right, you may suffer from highly distressing self-doubt almost all the time. Your fears and negative beliefs about yourself may cause you to miss opportunities, avoid challenges, and follow self-destructive patterns of behaviour. You tend to see difficulties in life as being central to your true self ('This is me.' 'This is how I am.'). So it is hard to step back far enough to see things clearly, or to work systematically to change things for the better. Working through these workbooks on your own may not enable you to dislodge your negative self-beliefs. You may also need help from a professional therapist.

Most people fall somewhere between these two extremes. If you are in this middle range, these workbooks will be particularly useful. You will be aware of your low self-esteem and wish to do something about it. You will also be able to stand back from the way you habitually see yourself and search for alternative perspectives. As you work through the books, you will begin to understand how your negative opinions developed, use close self-observation to change old thinking patterns, and replace those unhelpful beliefs with a new, more kindly, respectful and accepting view of yourself.

Summary

1 Self-esteem is the opinion you have of yourself, the judgements you make about yourself, and the value you place on yourself as a person.

2 'Low self-esteem' means having a poor opinion of yourself, judging yourself harshly and seeing yourself as having little worth or value.

3 At the heart of low self-esteem lie negative beliefs about yourself. These are reflected in how you behave on a day-to-day basis, and can affect many areas of life.

4 Low self-esteem can be a cause or an effect of a whole range of other difficulties.

5 The extent to which low self-esteem disrupts daily life varies from person to person.

SECTION 2: Understanding How Low Self-Esteem Develops

This section will help you understand:

- where beliefs about ourselves come from
- how low self-esteem develops
- how negative experiences affect people
- how negative experiences lead to your Bottom Line
- what biased thinking is
- what your Rules for Living are

Where do beliefs about ourselves come from?

At the heart of self-esteem lie your central beliefs about yourself. You may think of these beliefs as facts, reflections of the real truth about you. But beliefs are actually opinions rather than facts – and it's important to remember that opinions can be mistaken, biased, inaccurate or just plain wrong. And opinions can be changed.

Most people's ideas about themselves are based on the experiences they've had in their lives and the messages they've received about the kind of people they are.

If your experiences have generally been positive – if good things have happened to you, if you've been surrounded by loving family and friends, if you've done well at school and at work, been praised for your successes and your talents – then your beliefs about yourself are likely to be positive too.

If your experiences have been mixed – if for example you weren't the most popular person at school but then blossomed in your first job, if your first real love let you down but you then met a supportive and loving partner – then you may have a good opinion of yourself in some circumstances, but feel bad about yourself in others.

However if your experiences have been generally negative – at home as you were growing up, at school, at work, in relationships – then you may well have negative beliefs about yourself, leading to low self-esteem.

As you read through this section of the workbook, think about how the ideas might apply to you personally:

- What do you recognize from your own life?
- What helps you to make sense of how you feel about yourself?

- Which of the stories ring bells for you?

- What are the experiences that have contributed to low self-esteem in your own particular case?

Note down anything that occurs to you as you read – ideas, memories, hunches. The aim is to help you to understand why it is that you have low self-esteem. You will discover that your ideas about yourself are an understandable reaction to what has happened to you – that is, anyone with your life experience would probably hold similar views.

You will begin to see how conclusions you reached about yourself (perhaps many years ago) have influenced the way you have thought and felt and acted over time. This understanding is the first step towards change.

How does low self-esteem develop?

These are the ingredients that lead to low self-esteem:

Negative Early Experiences

Events, relationships, etc.

e.g. rejection, neglect, abuse, criticism and punishment,
lack of praise, interest, warmth or acceptance,
being the 'odd one out' in your family or at school

The Bottom Line

Negative conclusions about yourself, based on these experiences

e.g. 'I am bad', 'I am worthless', 'I am stupid', 'I am not good enough'

Rules for Living

Ways you think you should behave, because you believe the Bottom Line

e.g. 'I must always put others first', 'If I say what I think, I will be rejected',
'Unless I do everything to the highest possible standard, I will achieve nothing'

Trigger Situations

Situations in which the Rules for Living are (or may be) broken

e.g. being rejected, the possibility of failing, feeling that you might lose control

Negative Early Experiences can lead to a negative **Bottom Line** (negative beliefs about yourself). Because the **Bottom Line** seems to be true, rather than just a belief or opinion, we then adopt **Rules for Living** which are designed to help us get by, but in fact keep us stuck in low self-esteem. Then, when we find ourselves in a relevant **Trigger Situation** (for example, when we believe we have failed or think we might lose control), our **Bottom Line** is activated and we feel as if our negative beliefs about ourselves have been confirmed ('There you are, I *knew* it').

How do negative experiences affect people?

Beliefs about ourselves (and indeed about other people and about life) are all learned. They have their roots in experience. Your beliefs about yourself are conclusions you have reached on the basis of what has happened to you. This means that, however unhelpful or outdated they may now be, they are nonetheless understandable – there was a time when they made perfect sense, given what was going on in your life.

You can learn in many ways – from direct experience, from your own observation, from the media, from listening to what people around you say and watching what they do. Important experiences, which may help to form your beliefs about yourself, often occur early in life. What you saw, heard and experienced in childhood, in your family, at school and among your friends, will have influenced your thinking in ways that may have persisted to the present day.

Common Negative Experiences

As a child:

1 Were you regularly punished, neglected or abused?

2 Did you fail to meet your parents' standards?

3 Did you fail to meet your friends' standards?

4 Were you on the receiving end of other people's stress or distress?

5 Was your family or social group the target of prejudice?

continues on next page

> **6** Did you experience a lack of praise, affection, warmth and interest from others?
>
> **7** Were you the 'odd one out' at home?
>
> **8** Were you the 'odd one out' at school?
>
> Later on, as an adult:
>
> **9** Did you experience bullying at work, an abusive relationship, long-term stress or hardship, or major trauma?

Let's look at each of these issues in more detail, with some case studies about real people who have experienced these problems in their own lives.

1 Regular punishment, neglect or abuse

If children are treated badly, they often assume that they must have somehow deserved it. If you were frequently punished (especially if the punishment was excessive, unpredictable or made no sense to you), if you were neglected, abandoned or abused, these experiences will have influenced the way you see yourself.

CASE STUDY: Briony

Briony was adopted by her father's brother and his wife after both her parents were killed in a car crash when she was seven. Her new step-parents already had two older daughters. Briony became the family scapegoat. Everything that went wrong was blamed on her. Briony was a loving little girl, who liked to please people. She tried desperately to be good, but nothing worked. Every day she faced new punishments. She was deprived of contact with friends, made to give up music – which she loved – and was forced to do more than her fair share of work around the house. Briony became more and more confused. She could not understand why everything she did was wrong.

One night, when she was eleven, Briony's stepfather came silently into her room in the middle of the night. He put his hand over her mouth and raped her. He told her that she was dirty and disgusting, that she had asked for it, and that if she told anyone what had happened, no one would believe her, because they all knew she was a filthy little liar. Afterwards, she crept around the house in terror. No one seemed to notice or care. Briony's doubts about herself crystallized into a firm belief at that point. She was bad. Other people could see it, and would treat her accordingly.

2 Failing to meet parental standards

If others treated you as if nothing you did was good enough, focused on your mistakes at the expense of your successes, teased you, or made you feel small, all these experiences may have left you with the sense that there was something fundamentally wrong with you.

CASE STUDY: Jesse

Jesse's father was an insurance salesman. He had never realized his ambitions to rise to a manager's position, and put this down to the fact that his parents had failed to support him during his years at school. They had never seemed particularly interested in what he was doing, and it was easy to skip school and neglect his homework. He was determined not to make the same mistake with his own children. Every day, at the supper table, he would question them about what they had learned. Everyone had to have an answer, and the answer had to be good enough.

Jesse remembered dreading the sight of his father's car in the drive when he came home. It meant another grilling. He was sure his mind would go blank and he would be unable to think of anything to say. When this happened, his father's face would fall in disappointment. Jesse could see that he was letting his father down. He felt he fully deserved the close questioning that followed. 'If you can't do better than this,' his father would say, 'you'll never get anywhere in life.' In his heart of hearts, Jesse agreed. It was clear to him that he was not good enough: he would never make it.

3 Failing to meet your friends' standards

Children and young people can be powerfully influenced, not only by their parents' standards, but also by the demands of their friends. Particularly during adolescence, when you are developing your own personality and sexual identity, the pressure to fit in with others can be very strong. Feeling that you are failing to meet your friends' standards can be very painful and lonely, and may lead to low self-esteem.

CASE STUDY: Karen

Karen was an attractive, sturdy, energetic girl who enjoyed sport and loved dancing. She grew up at a time when the ideal body shape for women was to be tall and extremely slender. Although she was not at all overweight, Karen's natural body shape was not even close to this ideal. Her mother tried to boost her confidence by telling her that she was 'well built'. This clumsy attempt to help her to feel OK about herself backfired. 'Well built' was not what she was supposed to be. Karen's friends all loved fashion and spent hours shopping and trying on clothes. Karen would join them but, in the shared changing rooms common at the time, felt horribly self-conscious. Every mirror showed how far her body failed to meet the ideal. Her broad shoulders and rounded hips were just completely wrong.

Karen decided to diet. In the first two weeks, she lost a couple of kilos. Her friends thought she looked great. Karen was delighted. She continued to restrict her eating and to lose weight. But somehow, no matter how hard she tried, she could never be thin enough. And she was constantly hungry. In the end, she gave in and began to eat normally again, and then to over-eat. This was the beginning of a lifelong pattern of alternately dieting and overeating. Karen was never happy with her physical self. As far as she was concerned, she was fat and ugly.

4 Being on the receiving end of other people's stress or distress

Even in loving families, changes in circumstances can sometimes create distress which has a lasting impact on children. Parents who are stressed, unhappy or distracted may have little patience with normal naughtiness, or with a young child's natural lack of self-control and skill.

CASE STUDY: Geoff

Geoff was an energetic, adventurous, curious little boy. He had very little fear and, even as a toddler, was climbing trees and plunging into deep water without a second thought. His mother used to say she needed eyes in the back of her head to keep track of him. Geoff's parents were proud of his adventurousness, and found him funny and endearing.

When he was three, however, twin babies arrived. At the same time, Geoff's father lost his job and had to take work at a much lower rate of pay. The family moved from a house with a garden to a small apartment on the fourth floor of a large block. With two new babies, things were chaotic. Geoff's father felt his job loss keenly, and became gloomy and irritable. His mother was constantly tired. In the confined space of the apart-ment, there was nowhere for Geoff's energy to go, and his interest and curiosity only made a mess.

He became a target for anger and frustration. Because he was only little, he did not understand why this change had happened. He tried hard to sit quietly and keep out of trouble, but again and again he ended up being shouted at and sometimes smacked. It was no longer possible to be himself without being told he was a naughty, disobedient boy. Even as an adult, whenever he met with disapproval or criticism, he still felt the old sense of despair that he would never be accepted.

5 Feeling that your family or social group is the target of prejudice

Your beliefs about yourself may not simply be based on how you personally were treated. Sometimes low self-esteem is partly caused by the way a person and his or her family live, or by his or her identity as a member of a group. If, for example, your family was very poor, if your parents had serious difficulties which meant the neighbours looked down on them, if you were a member of a racial, cultural or religious group which was a focus for hostility, these experiences may have left you feeling inferior to other people.

CASE STUDY: Arran

Arran was the middle one of seven children, in a family of travellers. He was brought up by his mother and his maternal grandmother and had no long-term father figure. Arran's grandmother, a striking woman with bleached hair, coped by drinking. Arran had clear memories of being rushed through the streets to school, his grandmother pushing two babies crammed into a buggy, the older children and another whining toddler trailing behind. Lack of money meant that all the children wore second-hand clothes, which were passed down from one to the next. Their sweatshirts were grubby, their shoes scuffed, their faces smudged, their hair standing on end. Every so often, the grandmother would stop and screech at the older children to hurry up.

What stuck in Arran's mind was the faces of people coming in the opposite direction as they saw the family approaching. He would see their mouths twist, their disapproving frowns, their eyes looking away. He could hear their muttered comments to one another. The same happened when they reached the school. In the playground, other children and their parents kept away from him and his family.

Arran's grandmother, too, was well aware of other people's attitude. She was fiercely protective of the family, in her own way. She would shout and swear, calling names and screaming threats.

Throughout his schooldays, Arran felt a deep sense of shame. He saw himself as a worthless outcast, whose best form of defence was attack. He was constantly fighting other kids, didn't concentrate in lessons, left with no qualifications, and spent his time with other young men who were involved in petty crime. The only time he felt good about himself was when he had successfully broken the rules – perhaps stolen something without being caught or beaten someone up without being punished.

6 Experiencing a lack of praise, affection, warmth and interest from others

It is easy to see how abuse or prejudice could contribute towards someone feeling bad, inferior, weak or unlovable. But sometimes the important experiences are less obvious. If you had a fairly settled, normal childhood, how come you have so much trouble believing in your own worth?

Perhaps the problem was an *absence* of the day-to-day good things that make a person feel accepted and valued? Perhaps, for example, you did not receive *enough* interest, *enough* praise and encouragement, *enough* warmth and affection? Perhaps in your family, although there was no actual unkindness, love and appreciation were not directly expressed? If so, this could have influenced your ideas about yourself.

CASE STUDY: Kate

Kate was brought up by elderly, middle-class parents. At heart, both were good people who tried their best to give their only daughter a sound start in life. However, they both had difficulty in openly expressing affection. Their only means of showing how much they loved her was through caring for her practical needs. So, they were good at ensuring that Kate did her homework, in seeing that she ate a balanced diet, that she was well dressed and had a good range of books and toys.

As she grew older, they made sure she went to a good school, took her to girl guides and swimming lessons, and paid for her to go on holiday with friends. But they almost never touched her – there were no cuddles, no kisses, no pet names. At first, Kate was hardly aware of this. But once she began to see how openly loving other families were, she began to experience a sad emptiness at home. She did her best to change things. She would take her father's hand as they walked along – but noticed how he would drop it as soon as he decently could. She would put her arms round her mother – and feel how she stiffened. She tried to talk about how she felt, but her parents quickly changed the subject.

Kate concluded that their behaviour must reflect something about her. Her parents did their duty by her, but no more. It must mean she was fundamentally unlovable.

7 Being the 'odd one out' at home

Another factor that can contribute to low self-esteem is the experience of being the 'odd one out'. Perhaps you were an artistic child in an academic family? Or you may have been an energetic, sporty child in a quiet family? There was nothing particularly wrong with you, or with them, but for some reason you did not fit the family norm. Other family members may only have teased you in a good-natured way or perhaps expressed mild puzzlement. But you could still have ended up with a sense that being different from the norm means being odd, unacceptable or inferior.

CASE STUDY: Sarah

Sarah was an exceptional artist. However, both her parents were teachers who thought that academic achievement was the most important thing in life. They were plainly delighted with her two older brothers, who did very well at school and became a doctor and a lawyer. Sarah, however, was an average student. There was nothing particularly wrong with her schoolwork – she simply did not shine as her parents hoped she would.

Her real talent lay in her hands and eyes. She could draw and paint, and her collages were full of energy and colour. Sarah's parents tried to appreciate her artistic gifts, but they saw art and craft work as essentially a waste of time. They never openly criticized her. But she could see how their faces lit up when they heard about her brothers' achievements, while showing little enthusiasm when she brought her artwork home. They always seemed to have more important things to do than look carefully at what she had done ('Very nice, dear').

Sarah concluded that she was inferior to other, cleverer people. As an adult, she found it difficult to take pleasure in her artistic talent, tended to apologize for her work, and fell silent in the company of anyone she saw as more intelligent or educated than herself.

8 Being the 'odd one out' at school

In the same way that not fitting into your family can make it difficult to feel good about yourself, so being in some way different from others at school can lead people to see themselves as weird or inferior. Children and young people who stand out from the group can be cruelly teased and left out. For many children – whether it's having a different skin colour, wearing spectacles, being shy, having a different accent, being very good at school work or being very slow to learn – being different is wrong. Did you feel like the 'odd one out' at school because of your appearance, personality or abilities?

CASE STUDY: Chris

Chris's early childhood was happy. But he began to experience difficulties as soon as he went to school, because of undiagnosed dyslexia. While all the other children in the class seemed to be racing ahead with their reading and writing, he lagged behind. He just could not get the hang of it. He was assigned a teacher to give him special help, and had to keep a special home reading record which was different from everyone else's.

Other children started to laugh at him and call him 'thicko' and 'dumbo'. He made up for this by becoming the class clown. He was the one who would always get involved in silly pranks. The teachers began to lose patience with him, and to label his difficulties laziness and attention-seeking. When his parents were called to the school yet again to discuss his behaviour, his comment to them was: 'What can you expect? I'm just stupid.'

9 Problems in adulthood

Although low self-esteem is often rooted in childhood or adolescent experiences, later experiences can also have a big impact. Even confident people, with strongly positive views of themselves, can have their self-esteem weakened by things that happen later in life. Examples include being bullied at work, being trapped in an abusive marriage, being ground down by a long period of stress or financial hardship, or experiencing a major trauma.

CASE STUDY: Jim

Jim was a fireman. As part of his job, he had attended many accidents and fires, and saved several people's lives. He had a stable, happy childhood and felt loved by both his parents. He saw himself as strong, and able to deal with anything life might throw at him. This was why he was able to remain outgoing and cheerful, despite his risky and demanding job.

One day, as he was driving down a busy street, a woman stepped off the pavement immediately in front of him, and was caught under the wheels of his car. By the time he was able to stop, she had been fatally injured. Jim always carried a first aid kit, and he got out of the car to see what he could do. After a while, however, during which other people had called an ambulance and gathered round to help, he felt increasingly sick and shocked and retreated to his car.

Like many people who have suffered or witnessed horrific accidents, Jim later began to suffer symptoms of post-traumatic stress. He kept replaying the accident in his mind. He was tormented by guilt – he should have been able to stop the car, he should have stayed with the victim to the bitter end. He was constantly tense, irritable and miserable.

Jim's usual way of coping with difficulties was to tell himself that life goes on, that he must put it behind him. So he tried not to think about what had happened. Unfortunately, this made it impossible for him to come to terms with it. He began to feel that his personality had changed. The fact that he had not been able to prevent the accident, that he had withdrawn to the car, and that he could not control his feelings meant that, far from being the strong, competent person he had believed himself to be, he was actually weak and inadequate – a nervous wreck.

How do negative experiences lead to your Bottom Line?

As people grow up, they continue to hear, in their minds, the voices of people who were important to them. Parents, grandparents, older brothers or sisters, teachers, child-minders, friends and schoolmates can all have a major impact on self-confidence and self-esteem. We may criticize ourselves in their exact, sharp tones, call ourselves the same unkind names.

We may experience emotions and body sensations from an earlier time in our lives, and see images in our mind's eye of events that occurred many years ago. Sarah, for example, when she submitted a painting for exhibition, would hear her mother's patient voice ('Well, I suppose if *you* like it, dear') and experience the same sinking feeling in her stomach that she experienced as a child. Geoff, when in the best of spirits and full of energy, would suddenly catch a flash in his mind's eye of his father's shouting, angry face and feel instantly in the wrong.

Why is this? How come these events, which happened so long ago, still influence how we feel and think and act in the present?

The answer lies in the way that our experiences have led us to make judgements about ourselves as people. These judgements form 'The Bottom Line'. The Bottom Line is the view of yourself that lies at the heart of low self-esteem. It can often be summed up in a single sentence, beginning with the words, 'I am…'

To get a sense of what this means, look back over the case studies you have just read and see if you can match the Bottom Lines on the left on p. 22 with the names of the people on the right. Draw a line linking the name of each person with his or her Bottom Line (cover up the real answers just below before you do this):

I am stupid	**Karen**
I am bad	**Jim**
I am fat and ugly	**Briony**
I am worthless	**Kate**
I am not good enough	**Chris**
I am unlovable	**Sarah**
I am not important	**Geoff**
I am a nervous wreck	**Arran**
I am unacceptable	**Jesse**

Here are their actual Bottom Lines:

Briony:	*I am bad*
Jesse:	*I am not good enough*
Karen:	*I am fat and ugly*
Geoff:	*I am unacceptable*
Arran:	*I am worthless*
Kate:	*I am unlovable*
Sarah:	*I am not important*
Chris:	*I am stupid*
Jim:	*I am a nervous wreck*

The negative ideas that these people developed about themselves made perfect sense to them, given their experiences. But, when you read their stories, did you agree with their opinions? Did *you* think that:

- Briony was bad?
- Jesse was a failure?
- Karen was fat and ugly?
- Geoff was always in the wrong?

- Arran deserved to be an outcast?

- Kate was unlovable?

- Sarah was unimportant?

- Chris was stupid?

- Jim was inadequate and weak, a nervous wreck?

As an outsider, you could probably see that Briony was not responsible for what her stepfather did to her, that Jesse's father's own needs were clouding his judgement, that Karen's only shortcoming was not meeting a false ideal, that Geoff's parents changed towards him because their difficult circumstances made them lose sight of his lovable qualities. You probably also realized that the disapproval Arran attracted as a small child was not his fault, that it was Kate's parents' own limitations that prevented them from being more loving towards her, that Sarah's parents' narrow standards prevented them from enjoying her artistic gifts, that Chris's slowness to learn was nothing to do with stupidity, and that Jim's distress was an understandable reaction to a horrific event and not a sign of weakness or inadequacy.

Now think about your own view of yourself and the experiences that have helped to create it, both while you were growing up and perhaps also later in your life. Use these questions to help you to put your own Bottom Line into words.

1 What do you say about yourself when you are being self-critical?

_____

_____

_____

_____

_____

2 What names do you call yourself when you are angry and frustrated?

_____

_____

_____

_____

3 What were the words people in your life used to describe you when they were angry, or disappointed in you?

_____

_____

_____

_____

4 What messages about yourself did you pick up from your parents, other members of your family or your friends?

_____

_____

_____

_____

5 If you could express your Bottom Line in a single 'I am…' sentence, what would it be?

_____

_____

_____

_____

_____

6 What experiences is this opinion based on? What comes to mind when you think back to when you first felt this way about yourself? Did a single event, or a series of events over time, form your ideas? Or was there a general atmosphere – perhaps of coldness or disapproval?

_____

_____

_____

_____

_____

_____

_____

Make a note of your ideas. You will be able to use this information later on to help you find a more helpful perspective on yourself.

Understanding the origins of low self-esteem is the first step towards change. You can probably see that the conclusions Briony and the others reached about themselves were based on misunderstandings about the meanings of their experiences – misunderstandings that made perfect sense at the time, given that they were children, with no adult knowledge on which to base a broader, more realistic view. Or, in Jim's case, too distressed to think straight about himself.

It's worth remembering...

However powerful and convincing your Bottom Line may seem, it is usually biased and inaccurate, often because it is based on a child's eye view.

Think about your own Bottom Line.

- Are your own negative ideas about yourself based on similar misunderstandings?

_____

_____

_____

_____

_____

- Have you blamed yourself for something that was not your fault?

_____

_____

_____

_____

- Have you taken responsibility for someone else's behaviour?

_____

_____

_____

_____

- Have you seen specific problems (for example, difficulty asserting yourself) as a sign that you are a person of little worth?

_____

_____

_____

_____

_____

- Did you accept other people's standards before you were experienced enough to see their limitations and question them?

_____

_____

_____

_____

_____

- If another person had had your experiences, would you judge them as negatively as you do yourself? Or would you come to different conclusions?

_____

_____

_____

_____

- How would you understand and explain what happened to you, if it had happened to someone you respected and cared about rather than to yourself?

_____

_____

_____

_____

You may not find it easy at first to answer these questions, so take your time and come back to them more than once if you find that helpful.

Once the Bottom Line is in place, it can be very difficult to stand back from it and question it. This is because the Bottom Line is strengthened by biased thinking, which makes you home in on anything that supports your negative conclusions, while encouraging you to screen out anything that does not support them.

What is biased thinking?

Biased thinking means always looking at yourself, and interpreting what you see, in a negative way.

Biased perception (focusing on weaknesses and ignoring strengths)

If your self-esteem is low, you are probably quick to notice anything about yourself that you do not like. It could be a physical feature (e.g. 'My eyes are too small'), your character (e.g. 'I wish I wasn't so shy') or a mistake that you make (e.g. 'Not again.

How *could* I be so stupid?'). On the other hand, you may find it hard to notice anything good about yourself. So whenever you think about your looks, character or behaviour, you home in on your weaknesses and ignore your strengths. The end result is that you keep focusing on what you think is wrong with you, and not on what is right.

To see how this applies to you, think back over the last week or two and write down three occasions when you focused on a weakness or ignored a strength (there is an extra page at the back of this book if you need it):

1 _____

_____

_____

_____

_____

2 _____

_____

_____

_____

_____

3 _____

_____

_____

_____

_____

Biased interpretation (always seeing the downside)

Low self-esteem not only unbalances what you notice about yourself, it also changes the way you interpret what happens to you. If something does not go well, you may use it as the basis for a general judgement about yourself (e.g. 'Typical, I always get it wrong'). So even quite small mistakes can appear to reflect your entire worth as a person. Even neutral and positive experiences can be twisted to fit a biased, negative view of yourself. For example, if someone compliments you on looking well, you may think 'Hmm, then I must have been looking pretty bad up till now'. Or you may dismiss the compliment altogether (e.g. 'They were only being kind – they just feel sorry for me'). This sort of biased interpretation always favours self-criticism, not self-acceptance or self-appreciation.

Write down three recent occasions when you twisted something that happened to fit your view of yourself (again, there is an extra page at the back of the workbook if you need it):

1 _____

_____

_____

_____

2 _____

_____

_____

_____

3 _____

_____

_____

_____

> ## It's worth remembering...
>
> **Biased perception and biased interpretation work together to support and strengthen your Bottom Line.**

The end result

Negative beliefs and biased thinking trap you in a vicious circle, as you can see from the diagram below. Given your negative beliefs about yourself, you tend to assume that events will turn out badly. This assumption makes you sensitive to any sign that things are indeed turning out as you predicted. In addition, no matter how things turn out, you are likely to see them in a negative way. Because of this, your memories of what happened will also be negatively biased. This strengthens your negative beliefs, and sets you up to continue to assume the worst.

Biased thinking: a vicious circle

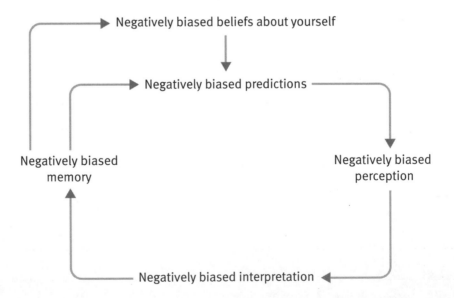

Biased thinking prevents you from realizing that your Bottom Line is an opinion, not a fact. It keeps your negative views in place, makes you anxious and unhappy, restricts your life and prevents you from finding a more balanced and accurate view of yourself.

What are your Rules for Living?

Even if you believe yourself to be incompetent or inadequate, unattractive or unlovable, you still have to get on with life. Rules for Living help you to do this. They allow you to feel reasonably comfortable with yourself, so long as you obey them.

However they also help to keep the Bottom Line in place and so maintain low self-esteem. Let's think back to the people in the case studies mentioned earlier and see how each one's Bottom Line fits with the Rule for Living written in his or her thought bubble. How do they think they should behave, assuming their central ideas about themselves to be true?

Bottom Line	**Rules for Living**
Briony → *'I am bad'* →	'If I allow anyone to get close to me, they will hurt and exploit me.'
Jesse → *'I am not good enough'* →	'Unless I always get it right, I will never get anywhere in life.'
Karen → *'I am fat and ugly'* →	'My worth depends on how I look and what I weigh.'
Geoff → *'I am unacceptable'* →	'I must always keep myself under tight control.'
Arran → *'I am worthless'* →	'No matter what I do, no one will accept me.'
Kate → *'I am unlovable'* →	'Unless I do everything people expect of me, I will be rejected.'
Sarah → *'I am not important'* →	'If someone is not interested in me, it is because I am unworthy of interest.'
Chris → *'I am stupid'* →	'It's better not to try than to fail.'
Jim → *'I am a nevous wreck'* →	'Letting my emotions get the better of me is a sign of weakness.'

Because they believe their Bottom Lines are true, each of these people has developed Rules for Living to help them get by. For example, Briony believed she was bad – and therefore deserved to be treated badly. So she decided not to have close relationships, in order to avoid the possibility of being hurt.

To some extent, Rules for Living work. For example, Jesse's high standards and fear of failure motivated him to perform very well, and enabled him to be very successful in his career. But he paid a price for this. His Rules for Living created an increasing sense of strain, and made it impossible for him to relax and enjoy his achievements. In addition, his need to perform well meant that work dominated his life, at the expense of personal relationships and leisure time.

- What are your Rules for Living? (You may have two or three so extra pages have been provided at the back of the workbook.)

_____

_____

_____

_____

_____

_____

- Think about each of your Rules and write down how each one helps you in life.

_____

_____

_____

_____

_____

_____

_____

_____

● Now write down how each Rule restricts you in your life.

_____

_____

_____

_____

_____

_____

_____

In Part Three, you will find more details about Rules for Living, their impact on your thoughts and feelings and how you manage your life, and how to change them and liberate yourself from the demands they place upon you.

Summary

1 Your negative beliefs about yourself (your Bottom Line) are opinions, not facts.

2 They are conclusions about yourself based on experience (usually, but not necessarily, early experience). Many different experiences (e.g. abuse, hardship, lack of interest or absence of affection) can contribute to them.

3 Once in place, the Bottom Line can be hard to change. This is because it is supported and strengthened by biased thinking. Biased thinking emphasizes experiences that support the Bottom Line, while ignoring experiences that contradict it.

4 The Bottom Line leads you to develop Rules for Living (guidelines which you think you must obey in order to feel comfortable with yourself). These are designed to help you get through life. But in fact they keep your Bottom Line in place and maintain low self-esteem.

SECTION 3: What Keeps Low Self-Esteem Going?

This section will help you to understand:

- which situations trigger your Bottom Line and lead you down anxious or depressed paths

- what anxious predictions are

- how you react to anxious predictions

- how you get the feeling that your Bottom Line has been confirmed

- how self-critical thoughts affect you

- how to draw your own vicious circles, investigating what keeps your low self-esteem going

In this section, we will look at the vicious circles that are triggered when you find yourself in a situation in which you fear that you *might* have broken your Rules for Living, or believe that you *have* done so. These are the situations that will activate your Bottom Line.

As we have seen, Rules for Living help to keep low self-esteem at bay in the short term. However, in the long term, they actually keep it going because they make impossible demands – such as perfection, endless approval from others, or complete control over yourself or your world. Because your well-being depends on following these Rules, it becomes very fragile. If you find yourself in danger of breaking the Rules (e.g. there is a risk of being disliked or of losing control), or believe that you have done so (e.g. someone *did* dislike you, you *did* lose control), then the Bottom Line, which your Rules have protected you against, may rear its ugly head. Then you will begin to feel anxious, insecure or (if you are convinced your Rules *have* been broken) depressed.

The Bottom Line vicious circle

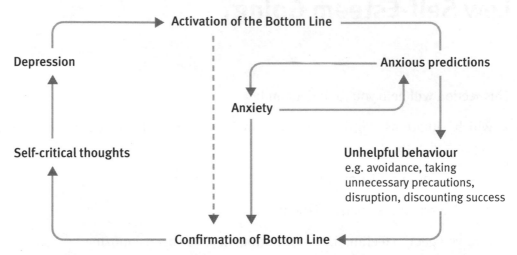

e.g. 'I knew it', 'I really am bad, worthless, stupid, not good enough, etc.'

You may find it helpful to keep a pen and paper beside you as you read through this section. Use the ideas described as an opportunity to deepen your understanding of how low self-esteem affects you in everyday life. Keep asking yourself:

- How does this fit with my experience?

- What situations trigger my anxious predictions?

- How do my predictions affect my emotions and my body state?

- What do I do (or not do) to stop them coming true?

- How do I feel when I think they have come true, and it seems as if my Bottom Line has been confirmed?

- What sort of self-critical thoughts do I have?

- How do these self-critical thoughts affect my feelings, my behaviour and my beliefs about myself?

Which situations trigger your Bottom Line?

The situations that trigger your Bottom Line depend on exactly what it is, and also on the Rules for Living you have developed to cope with it.

Think back to the people you met in Section 2. The situations that triggered their Bottom Lines were closely linked to their beliefs about themselves, and to their Rules for Living:

Person	Trigger situations
Briony:	Feeling that her true (bad) self might be revealed
Jesse:	Feeling that he might be unable to meet the high standards he had set himself, or being criticized by someone else
Karen:	Noticing that she had gained weight, or needing to buy clothes and fearing that she might attract stares or not fit into the size she thought she should be
Geoff:	Feeling very energetic or emotional, or being disapproved of
Arran:	Feeling vulnerable to attack or rejection, including in close relationships
Kate:	Being unable to do what was expected of her, or having to ask for help
Sarah:	Showing her work in public
Chris:	Having to write, especially if he had to do it in front of other people, or having to face any challenge (especially any intellectual challenge)
Jim:	Noticing signs that he was still upset and not his normal self

So the situations that activate your Bottom Line are those in which you think the Rules *might* be broken (there is an element of uncertainty) or definitely *have* been broken (you are quite sure). These are situations that cast doubt on the value you place on yourself as a person. They may be quite big events (e.g. losing a job, having a serious illness, a relationship breaking up). Or they may be little, everyday 'ups and downs' that you barely even notice. In order to understand what keeps your poor opinion of yourself going, you need to learn to recognize the changes in your mood that tell you that your Bottom Line has been activated.

Think back over the last week:

1 Note down any situations when you felt anxious, uncomfortable, depressed, or doubtful about your ability to handle what was going on.

_____

_____

_____

_____

_____

2 Note down any situations when you suspected that you were not making the impression you wanted to make.

_____

_____

_____

_____

_____

_____

3 Note down any situations when you felt that things were getting on top of you.

_____

_____

_____

_____

_____

_____

4 Do you notice any similarities between these situations?

_____

_____

_____

_____

_____

5 If so, what do they tell you about your own personal Rules for Living? What do you have to do or be in order to feel OK about yourself?

_____

_____

_____

_____

_____

_____

6 What Rules did you think you were breaking, or in danger of breaking?

_____

_____

_____

_____

_____

_____

7 What ideas about yourself came into your mind at these times?

_____

_____

_____

_____

_____

_____

8 Did you use any critical words to describe yourself? What were they? They may reflect your central negative beliefs about yourself (your Bottom Line).

_____

_____

_____

_____

_____

_____

_____

When the rules *might* be broken: the anxious path

Anxious predictions

When you are in a trigger situation that activates your Bottom Line because you fear your Rules *might* be broken, you start to worry about what may happen. These worries are your anxious predictions.

For example, imagine that you have to give a talk to a group of people – perhaps to colleagues at work, students in a class, or members of your church. Most people find this kind of situation rather anxiety-provoking. What is *your* immediate reaction when you imagine having to stand up and speak? Tick the answer/s that most closely match your own anxious predictions:

1 What thoughts come to mind?

☐ **a** 'I couldn't do it.'

☐ **b** 'I'd make a total fool of myself.'

☐ **c** 'No one would want to listen to me.'

☐ **d** 'I'd get so anxious I would have to run out.'

2 How do you imagine the audience reacting?

☐ **a** 'They would probably gaze out of the window and look bored.'

☐ **b** 'I'm worried that they would think I was weird.'

☐ **c** 'They might sit there smiling kindly, while secretly thinking what a sad case I was.'

☐ **d** 'I'm sure they would be disappointed because I wouldn't live up to their expectations.'

3 How do you imagine yourself reacting physically?

☐ **a** 'I know I'd go red in the face.'

☐ **b** 'My hands would feel sweaty.'

☐ **c** 'My mouth would probably go dry.'

☐ **d** 'My heart would be racing.'

☐ **e** 'All the muscles in my face would tense up.'

☐ **f** 'I'd have butterflies in my stomach.'

In challenging situations, a person with low self-esteem naturally assumes that the worst will happen and makes lots of anxious predictions. The anxious predictions make them frightened, with all the physical symptoms that go with that, and add to the stress of the situation.

How do you react to anxious predictions?

Anxious predictions may lead you to:

1 Avoid challenging situations

2 Take unnecessary precautions

3 Place too much weight on minor disruptions in your performance

4 Discount success

Unhelpful behaviour

1 Avoiding challenging situations

If you believe your anxious predictions strongly enough, you might decide to avoid the situation altogether. For instance, you might phone the person who had organized your presentation and tell them you had flu and would not be able to make it. Or you might simply not turn up.

How would you avoid giving a presentation? What excuses would you make?

_____

_____

_____

_____

_____

_____

Unfortunately, avoiding the situation would prevent you from finding out for yourself whether or not your anxious predictions were in fact correct. Things might actually have gone much better than you predicted.

So, in order to develop your confidence in yourself and your self-esteem, you need to begin approaching situations that you have been avoiding. Otherwise you will never gain the information you need to have a realistic, positive perspective on yourself.

2 Taking unnecessary precautions

Rather than avoiding the situation altogether, you might decide to give your talk, but take lots of precautions in order to ensure that your worst fears did not come true. For example, you might spend much longer than necessary rehearsing your presentation so as to be sure you got it right in every detail. Or you might avoid making eye contact with the audience, in case you saw them looking bored. Or you might leave no time for questions at the end – in case you were unable to answer them.

If you had to give a public presentation, what precautions would you take – in order to ensure that your worst fears were not realized?

_____

_____

_____

_____

_____

The problem with taking precautions is that (like avoidance) they prevent you from finding out whether your fears are actually true, or not. Instead, you are left with the sense that you had a narrow escape – your success (and so your feeling of self-worth) was entirely due to the precautions you took.

So, in order to become more confident, you need to approach challenging situations without taking precautions. Only by doing this will you discover that your precautions are unnecessary – you can get what you want out of life, and be the kind of person you want to be, without them.

3 Placing too much weight on minor disruptions in your performance

Sometimes performance is genuinely disrupted by anxiety. While giving your presentation, for example, you might find yourself stammering, your notes might shake in your hand, or your mind might go blank. These things happen, even to experienced speakers.

If your performance was disrupted by anxiety, what would your reaction be? What thoughts might come into your mind?

_____

_____

_____

_____

Self-confident people might notice these signs of anxiety and simply see them as an understandable reaction to being under pressure. They might believe that being nervous under these circumstances was quite normal, and be pretty sure that their anxiety was much less obvious to other people than it was to them. As far as confident people are concerned, being anxious does not matter particularly. They can accept a less than perfect performance, and they would not see it as reflecting on their worth as people. If you have low self-esteem, however, then you are likely to see any difficulties as evidence of your usual uselessness or incompetence. That is, they say something about you *as a person*.

So, to feel happier with yourself, you will need to start viewing your weaknesses simply as aspects of being a normal human being, rather than reasons to condemn yourself as a person.

4 Discounting success

Despite your anxieties, your presentation might have gone fine. Perhaps you said what you wanted to say, people seemed interested, you didn't get too nervous, there were some interesting questions, and you answered them well.

If this happened to you, would you give yourself a pat on the back? Or would you have a sneaking suspicion that you had done it by the skin of your teeth: the audience was just being kind, or you were lucky?

How would you react if your presentation went well? What kind of thoughts would come to mind?

_____

_____

_____

_____

_____

_____

_____

_____

Even when things go well, low self-esteem can remove your pleasure in what you achieve and make you likely to ignore or discount anything that does not fit your negative view of yourself (remember the negative biases in thinking that we described in Section 2 of this workbook).

So, learning to notice and take pleasure in your achievements and in the good things in your life is part of developing self-esteem. Part Three of the course will focus in detail on this.

How is your Bottom Line confirmed?

However you react to your anxious predictions, you will almost certainly end up feeling that your negative self-beliefs have been confirmed. You may actually say to yourself: 'There you are, I always knew it, I am simply not good enough' or you may just feel sad or gloomy, or have a sinking feeling in your stomach. Whatever form the sense of confirmation takes, the essential message is that what you always knew about yourself has been proved right, yet again.

How do self-critical thoughts affect you?

Once you believe that your negative ideas about yourself have been confirmed, you will probably react by criticizing and condemning yourself as a person. These self-critical thoughts may just flash briefly through your mind – or you may get trapped in a series of vicious attacks on yourself.

Here is what Jesse (the boy whose father quizzed him at the supper table) said to himself when his computer crashed and he lost an important document he was rushing to complete:

'Now look what you've done. You are a complete idiot. How could you be so stupid? You always mess things up – absolutely typical. You'll never amount to anything – you simply haven't got what it takes. Why are you always so useless?'

The computer crash wasn't actually Jesse's fault at all, but he still believed that it confirmed his negative ideas about himself. This made him angry and frustrated, and made it extremely difficult for him to calm down and work out how to solve the problem. It also made him think that he would always fail at everything in his life. This made him depressed. He had been due to go away at the weekend with some friends, but he couldn't face it. He sat around at home doing nothing in particular, worrying about the future. He couldn't see any real chance that things would ever change, so what was the point of carrying on?

Self-critical thoughts, like anxious predictions, have a major impact on how we feel and how we deal with our lives. They help to keep low self-esteem going. Think about your own reactions when things do not work out as you planned:

- What runs through your mind in these situations?

- Are you hard on yourself?

- Do you put yourself down and call yourself names, like Jesse?

- How do you feel when you are putting yourself down?

- Does it make it easier or harder for you to solve problems and tackle difficulties?

Being critical of yourself, especially if you believe that what you criticize in yourself cannot be changed, can pull you down into depression. This may be only a brief sadness, quickly banished by spending time with people you care about, or by engaging in an absorbing activity. Or it may develop into a longer-term condition. If this is the case for you, you may need to work on the depression in its own right before you begin to tackle low self-esteem (see p. xii for information on how to recognize depression that might need treatment).

Whether it is brief or longer-term, depression completes the vicious circle. Once you become depressed, the depression itself makes you more self-critical and more likely to see the future in a gloomy light. So depression keeps the Bottom Line activated, and encourages you to predict the worst. Bingo! You have a circular process that may continue, if you do not interrupt it, for long periods of time.

On the opposite page is the vicious circle Jesse drew up after his computer crashed.

Jesse's vicious circle

Trigger situation
Important assignment to complete for boss, to a tight deadline.
(Might break the rules by not being good enough, or attracting criticism)

Activation of the Bottom Line

Depression
Feel down, fed up with self.
Stay home, avoid everyone,
do nothing. Feel hopeless.

Anxious predictions
What if I don't get it done in time?
This has got to be 100 per
cent great – what if it's not
good enough? He'll be really
disappointed in me. I'm not
in good shape to do this.

Anxiety
Headachy, tense,
hands sweating,
churning stomach,
can't think straight.

Self-critical thoughts
Now look what you've done.
You are a complete idiot.
How could you be so stupid?

Unhelpful behaviour
Precautions: work all
the hours God sends.
Try to get every detail perfect.

Confirmation of Bottom Line
Computer crashes. Document lost. Sense of shock, dismay.
But not surprised. What else can I expect of myself?

When the rules definitely *have* been broken: the depressed path

When a person with low self-esteem believes that the Rules definitely *have* been broken, then rather than following the anxious path described above, he or she may immediately experience the sense that the Bottom Line has been confirmed – there is simply no doubt about it. In this case, there may be a short cut directly from activation to confirmation of the Bottom Line (see below), moving straight into self-criticism, hopelessness and depression, rather than experiencing the uncertainty reflected in the anxious path. This mini-vicious circle can then cycle on, keeping the person trapped in a low mood.

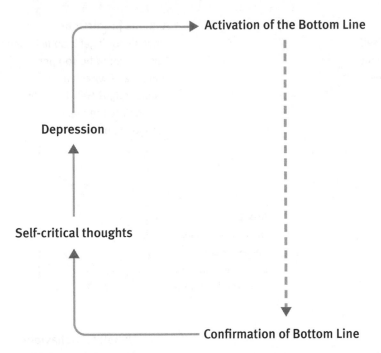

e.g. *'I knew it'*, *'I really am bad, worthless, stupid, not good enough, etc.'*

Jesse experienced this on another occasion at work. His boss made a passing remark about an error he had made on an assignment. Jesse's instant response was to see the remark as confirmation that he was indeed not good enough (his Bottom Line). Once again, he began to berate himself and his mood dipped. He forced himself to keep going to work, but felt dreadful for several days and even considered resigning.

How to draw your own vicious circle

As you have read through this workbook, you have been asked to consider how you personally might react in particular situations, to reflect on your own anxious predictions and their impact on your emotional state and your behaviour, your own sense that your negative beliefs about yourself have been confirmed, your own typical self-critical thoughts, and the impact these have on how you feel and how you manage your life.

Now you can fine-tune your observations by drawing up your own vicious circles in real life situations. You will find 'blanks' over the page (and additional blanks at the back of this book), which show the headings for each element of the anxious and depressed paths, and leave space for you to write. Here is a chance for you to find out more about the system when it is actually in operation, doing what it does.

- See if you can identify at least one situation over the next few days when you feel your Rules *might* be broken (you will know because you will feel anxious), and one when you believe they definitely *have* been broken (you will know because you will immediately feel down, rather than anxious).

- For each situation, follow the circle through, using the headings as a prompt to note your own personal experiences and reactions for each aspect of the circle.

- The exact flavour of the sequence is different from person to person, and indeed from situation to situation. So try to capture as precisely as you can your own anxious predictions (word for word, or perhaps images in your mind's eye), how you personally experience anxiety, what the sense of confirmation feels like for you, how you criticize yourself, how low mood affects you, and so on.

- Aim to record what you notice as soon as possible after it happens, so that it is still clear in your mind.

- If you wish, when you have completed one circle, you can repeat the process using a different trigger situation. Your task is to get curious about what keeps low self-esteem going – to be a detective, and ferret it all out.

Anxious vicious circle

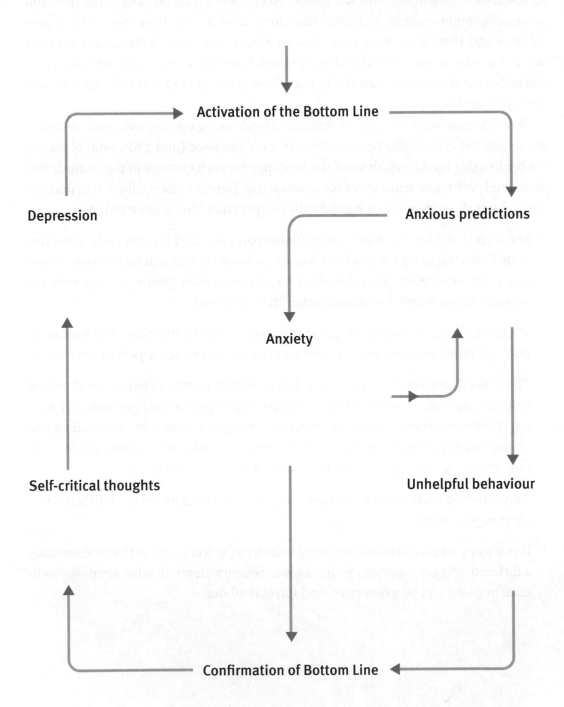

Trigger situation

Activation of the Bottom Line

Depression

Anxious predictions

Anxiety

Self-critical thoughts

Unhelpful behaviour

Confirmation of Bottom Line

Depressed vicious circle

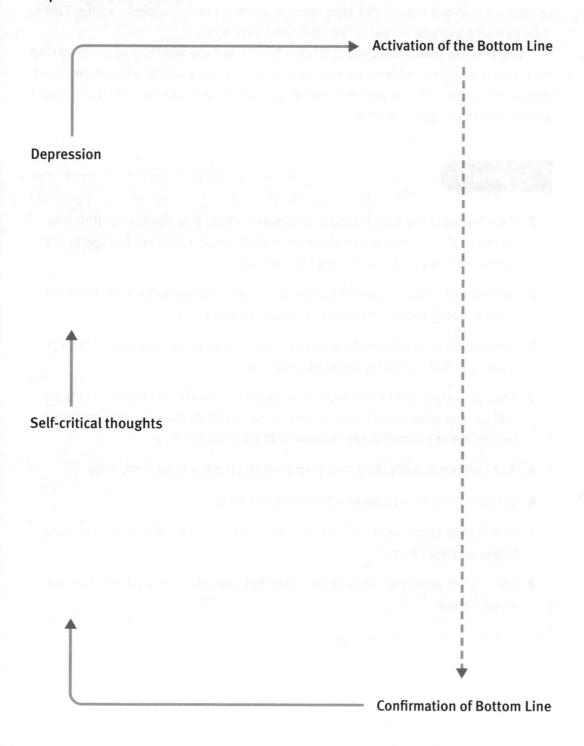

Activation of the Bottom Line

Depression

Self-critical thoughts

Confirmation of Bottom Line

Drawing your own vicious circles will increase your awareness of how your patterns of anxious and self-critical thinking operate to keep low self-esteem going. This is your first step towards breaking the circle and moving on.

In Part Two of this course, you will learn how to test the accuracy of your anxious predictions by approaching situations you normally avoid and dropping unnecessary precautions. You will also find out how to nip self-critical thinking in the bud, and how to weaken negative beliefs.

Summary

1 Your Bottom Line is activated in situations where you think your Rules for Living *might* be broken, or *have* been broken. Once activated, it triggers the vicious circles that keep low self-esteem going.

2 Uncertainty and self-doubt lead to negative predictions (expecting the worst and assuming there is nothing you can do to prevent it).

3 Negative predictions produce anxiety, with all its physical signs and symptoms (the body's normal response to threat).

4 They also affect your behaviour, leading you to avoid challenging situations and to take unnecessary precautions. Even if things go well, your negative beliefs about yourself make success difficult to accept.

5 The end result is a feeling that your Bottom Line has been confirmed.

6 Confirmation then triggers self-critical thinking.

7 Self-critical thinking often leads to a dip in mood, which may develop into a full-scale depression.

8 Low mood continues to activate your Bottom Line, thus completing the vicious circle.

Extra Charts and Worksheets

How does low self-esteem affect a person?

1 What did you talk about? (Did he or she express a lot of self-criticism, self-blame or self-doubt?)

_____

_____

_____

_____

_____

_____

_____

_____

_____

2 How did the person behave? (Did he or she sit hunched over, looking down? Did he or she speak in a hushed voice, or avoid making eye contact? Did you have the feeling he or she was putting on a front – working hard to appear cheerful, for example, or being the life and soul of the party instead of relaxing and being natural?)

_____

_____

_____

_____

_____

_____

_____

_____

_____

_____

3 **What sort of mood was the person in?** (For example, did he or she seem shy, sad, anxious, ashamed, frustrated or angry?)

_____

_____

_____

_____

_____

_____

_____

4 **How was the person's body state?** (For example, did he or she seem tired or tense?)

_____

_____

_____

_____

_____

_____

_____

Biased perception (focusing on weaknesses and ignoring strengths)

Think back over the last week or two and write down three occasions when you focused on a weakness or ignored a strength:

1 _____

_____

_____

_____

_____

_____

_____

2 _____

_____

_____

_____

_____

_____

_____

3 _____

_____

_____

_____

_____

_____

_____

Biased interpretation (always seeing the downside)

Write down three recent occasions when you twisted something that happened to fit your negative view of yourself:

1 _____

_____

_____

_____

_____

_____

_____

2 _____

_____

_____

_____

_____

_____

_____

3 _____

_____

_____

_____

_____

_____

_____

Rules for Living

- What are your Rules for Living?

- Think about each of your Rules and write down how each one helps you in life.

chart continues on next page

Rules for Living contd.

● Now write down how each Rule restricts you in your life.

Anxious vicious circle

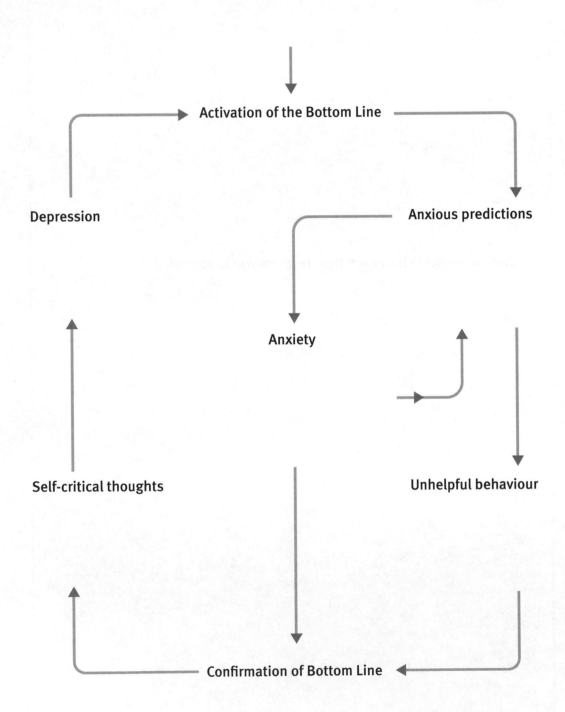

Anxious vicious circle

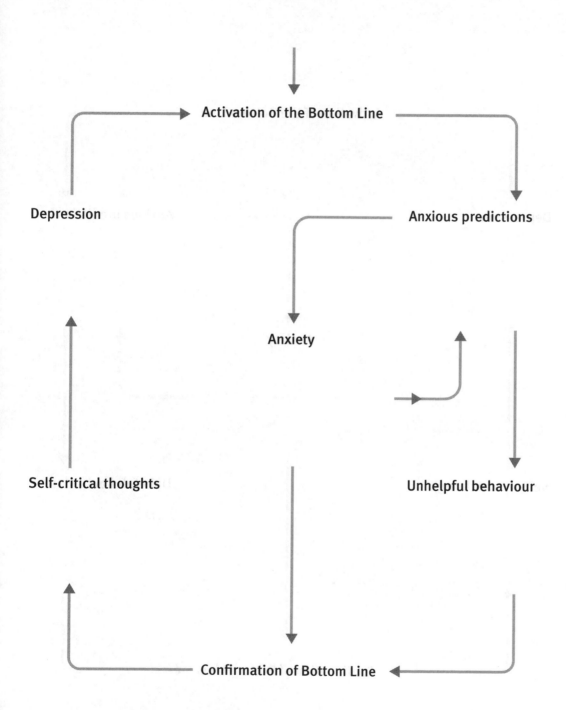

Anxious vicious circle

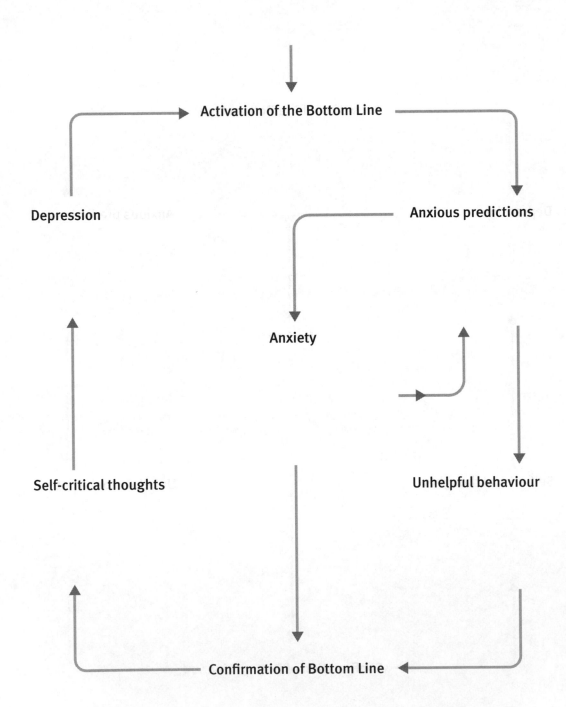

Trigger situation

Activation of the Bottom Line

Depression

Anxious predictions

Anxiety

Self-critical thoughts

Unhelpful behaviour

Confirmation of Bottom Line

Depressed vicious circle

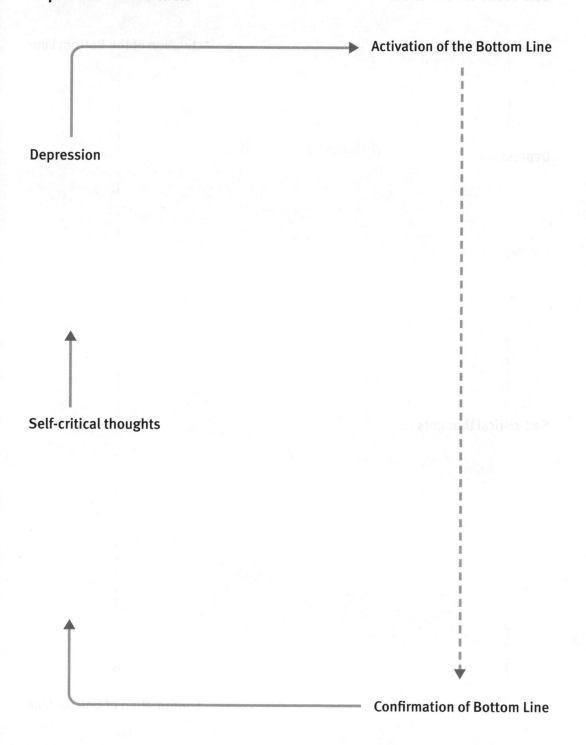

Activation of the Bottom Line

Depression

Self-critical thoughts

Confirmation of Bottom Line

Depressed vicious circle

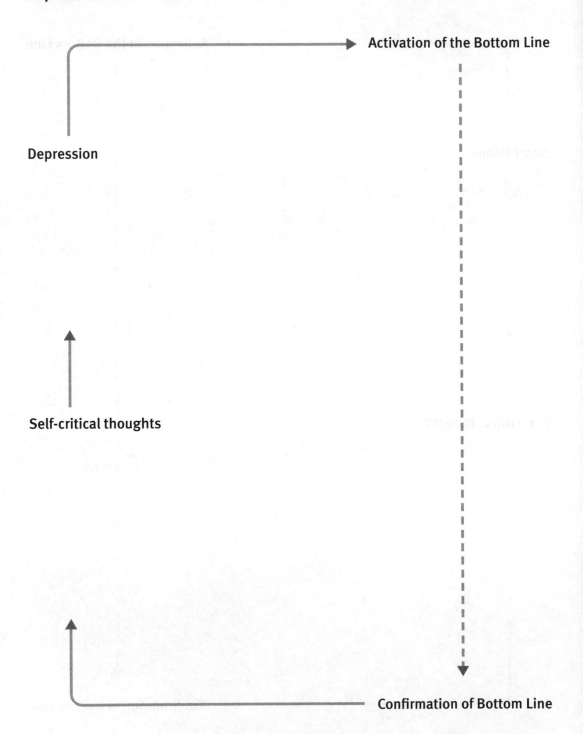

Activation of the Bottom Line

Depression

Self-critical thoughts

Confirmation of Bottom Line

Depressed vicious circle

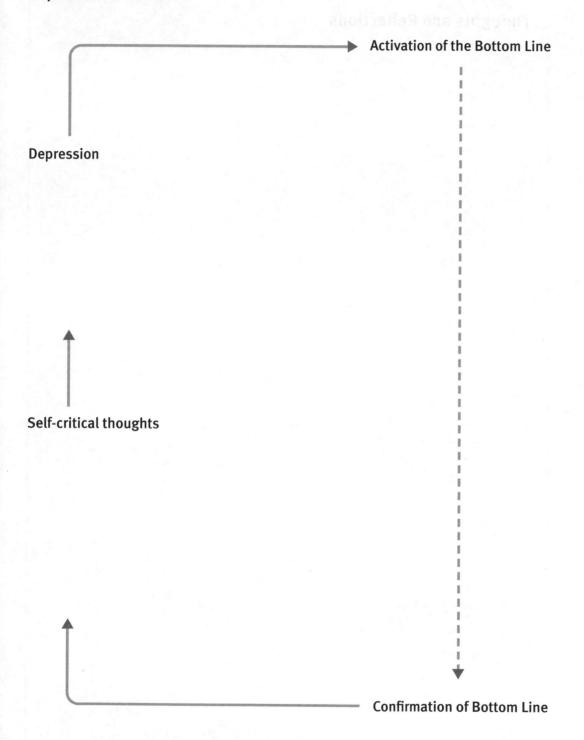

Activation of the Bottom Line

Depression

Self-critical thoughts

Confirmation of Bottom Line

Thoughts and Reflections

Thoughts and Reflections

68

Thoughts and Reflections